T0370503

Inspiration for Living Healthy and Well Through the Mind Body Spirit Connection

By
Dr. Ruth Joyce Colbert Barnes

AuthorHouse™
1663 Liberty Drive
Bloomington, IN 47403
www.authorhouse.com
Phone: 1 (800) 839-8640

Scripture taken from The Holy Bible, King James Version. Public Domain

Published by AuthorHouse   07/12/2018

ISBN: 978-1-5462-5004-3 (sc)
ISBN: 978-1-5462-5003-6 (e)

Library of Congress Control Number: 2018908086

Print information available on the last page.

This book is printed on acid-free paper.

Because of the dynamic nature of the Internet, any web addresses or links contained in this book may have changed
since publication and may no longer be valid. The views expressed in this work are solely those of the author and do
not necessarily reflect the views of the publisher, and the publisher hereby disclaims any responsibility for them.

Foreword

The courage and wisdom that it takes to cross over the bridge to gratefulness, hope and faith as it relates to health and a healthy lifestyle is dramatic at best.

The connection between mind, body and spirit and the acknowledgement of that phenomenal relationship is often not understood.

This book has a cadre of interrelationships and occurrences between the mind, body and spirit which clearly outlines and shows the magical, interesting, grand, magnetic connection among our physical reactions and our emotions.

This strong connection often times manifests its self through an un-answered healing process which occurs, I have been a health care professional for many years and I have observed and understand the connection between our bodies, our mind and the importance of our faith and spirit in healing.

Health prevention and a healthy lifestyle is truly the only way to concur anti-aging and longevity.

Anti-aging is certainly linked to the proper state of mind and our living activities.

The power of the mind, body and spirit helps to keep the body systems in sync. Clearly when the body just wants to give up on us, often times the mind and spirit will take over and give us the Grace, Peace, and Dignity that seems unexplainable to the Scientific mind.

This book represents a trilogy of books meant to inspire, motivate and empower the reader. They are filled with fun, good healthy advice, laughter, and tips for the reduction of the stresses in our lives and an exploration of the great adventure of living. In essence they are si-ne qua non to life.

Dedications

To my eternally great husband Joseph, who has always provided the love and support in my life and to the completion of great sweaters everywhere.

LOVE/Cleve RJ

This brief sharing of ideas is dedicated to my late mother Queenie Bell Colbert Joseph, who taught me at seven the proper graces, and the power of love, and faith, to Alisha Whetstone and especially to Jaime Moody.

Table of Contents

Introduction

Many years ago I learned at a very early age that life must be filled with great moments of abounding faith, empowering hope, and unselfish love. Life can often times bring disappointments and difficulties, when we are challenged with life's negative experiences we need to draw from deep within our spiritual being and find the peace that nurture's our heart and souls.

The Mind, Body and Spirit have such a magnificent connection which enables us to see and experience spirituality at work. Living healthy and well with the true spirit of this connection is a tremendous revelation. This connection allows us to appreciate the harmony in our lives, to live healthier, more inspired, more fulfilled lives.

Our world is filled with many modern devices, techniques, tools and equipment. However, only we are capable of grasping the opportunity of the Hope of every minute of life to be lived to the fullest.

Remember and understand that it is never too late for our dreams. The power is personal and within us. It is awesome and at the end of the day you are the one to make it happen.

—Ruth Joyce Colbert Barnes

CHAPTER
1

Chapter 1
Grateful Rewards

It is important in life to remember our blessings instead of focusing on negative things or what we are lacking. Write down the things that you are grateful for daily. This will affirm that you actually have more than what you believe.

Examples of my gratefulness *****:

- Grateful for the breath of life

- Grateful for the morning sunrise

- Grateful for spring flowers

- Grateful for loving relationships

- Grateful for clarity of mind

- Grateful for good health

- Grateful for the ability to speak and communicate

- Grateful for a real spiritual connection

- Grateful To think and reason clearly

- Grateful for good communication

- Grateful for my zoom transportation (sports car)

- Grateful for best, best friends

- Grateful for the sweetest family

- Grateful for the ocean & beach

- Grateful for beautiful artwork

- Grateful for summer's warmth

- Grateful for a beautiful waterfall

- Grateful for the snow peaked mountains

- Grateful for the Caribbean Sea

- Grateful for the look of a fresh blanket of snow

- Grateful for electronic technology "Wow"

- Grateful for my Pineapple Knock Down Cake

- Grateful for magic boo boo spray

- Grateful for the sheer joy of great grandchildren

- Grateful for beautiful memories

- Grateful for Tina Turner legs (you must think that you have them to know what I mean)

- Grateful for a cool breeze

- Grateful for a forest of trees

- Grateful for a great, noisy old man

- Grateful for really cool, black stretch pants

- Grateful for cool, clear water

- Grateful to have an appreciation for beautiful things

CHAPTER 2

Chapter 2
Self Awareness & Personal Happiness

The first rule for real happiness is self-awareness. To become aware of self allows you to become knowledgeable about your own likes and dislikes. Once you begin to understand more about yourself the things that you are passionate about will become apparent. Often we put a lot of effort into doing what others want us to do. If we wait around for others to make us happy or to be happy for us we will never truly be happy.

The essence of joy within oneself has to do with our choices; the basic ingredients are within us, within our reach, to be mastered. Personal happiness and joy within our inner self can be centered on our relationships with family, friends and acquaintances. A happy person must have goals, which will lead to actions and activities, that require a basic review of those goals on a regular basis.

We must learn to understand and appreciate what great things are right in front of us right now, at this moment. The way we think about circumstances which occur and the attitudes we display regarding these circumstances are directly associated with our good mental health, and living longer healthier lives.

There are many schools of thought which believe that our perceptions create contentment, anxiety or blissful characterizations within us. If this concept is correct then happiness has everything to do with encounters that we have. It is important for each of us to realize that we need to take a moment each day just for ourselves, you are a VIP (very important person), without you many things would not be accomplished. Most of us are caregivers for others; however we need to care for ourselves. Treat yourself like a VIP.

How many burdens have you eased for someone else? How much happiness have you brought to someone? What dreams have you pushed or encouraged for others? Remember you should treat yourself to some small indulgences each day to remind your- self that you are worth it and you do deserve the very best. This small gift to yourself will fortify you, arm you, and allow you to give more of yourself to others.

CHAPTER
3

Chapter 3

Renew, Refresh, Recharge, Utilizing The Colbert Center's "C-Zone Technique"

The key to maintaining and improving good emotional and physical health is to learn how to: refresh, relax, recharge and renew. We have developed a program at the Colbert Preventive Medicine Center which enables the patient to concentrate and focus on maintaining and improving optimal health.

The C-Zone Technique is unique to the Colbert Center; we encourage all of our patients and clients to focus on staying in the C-Zone and eliminate the impact of stress on your life. Many individuals are suffering from elevated cortisol levels and adrenal fatigue which release stimulation hormones.

These hormones affect our energy levels, food, cravings and weight gain. These hormones also begin the stress cycle.

The C-Zone categories include:

Corral the Challenges and distractions in your life identify the negative distraction and if possible rid yourself of them. Be prepared to make an opportunity from your challenges.

Cleanliness:

Hair

Skin

Nails

Feet

Body

We recommend special attention be given to all of the above referenced areas.

Carrots

Cabbage

Celery

Cucumbers

Cauliflower

Maintain a Calming State of Mind

Meditation

Yoga

Energy aura

Reading

Coping Strategies

- Visualization for relaxation

- Combat everyday stress by planning ahead

- Re-charge by eating- small snack protein based foods

- Soothing baths

- Walking with concentration and focus

Take a moment each day to care for yourself, identify creative opportunities, this approach to life will assist you in leading a more productive life. It will also assist you in solving difficult problems.

CHAPTER

4

Chapter 4
Dealing With Stress And Anxiety

Stress is described by some as excess pressure; it is different however from regular pressure. Stress occurs as a direct result of a lack of balance both emotionally and physically. The individual experiencing stress has developed poor ineffective coping strategies. We often ask ourselves, how did this happen? Stress manifests itself in various ways and often times the symptoms are severe. Some symptoms of stress include: insomnia, irritability, increased heart rate and increase in blood pressure.

These symptoms can be a result of the fast pace, critical issues occurring in life for everyone. Today, we are trying to do more and more with less support, less time, less money. These circumstances have made it easy to become overstressed.

Stress relief has a great deal to do with the status of your physical health. The status of your health can affect your mental state in a very significant way. The mind, body and spirit connection is a powerful force and when it is out of sync we can very often experience stress.

It is very necessary to learn how to deal effectively with all levels and sources of stress. Stress must be controlled because it can affect physical symptoms in a severe manner.

The following four methods of relaxation response are recommended for quick relief:

- Visualization technique

- Meditation

- Abdominal breathing

- Whole body release technique, pin pointing the areas of tension

"Methods of Relaxation"

Visualization Technique

Visualization is the ability to achieve a clear concise, mental depiction of anything. It can be a very positive method of seeing, focusing and understanding your goals, objectives, and capabilities. It can serve as a great reality check also, helping you to assess where you are or what your current status really is.

The skills needed for visualization is concentrated focus, be creative, focused and know your goals and desires. It can be a very powerful technique.

Meditation

This is a conscious exercise and method of relaxation which is geared toward calmness and peace, usually done in conjunction with guided breathing techniques.

It takes the correct environment, the correct attitude, the correct behavior to truly achieve the refreshed peace and good well-being which can be reached through deep practiced meditation. There is positive clean energy placed out into the universe when meditating. It takes around ten minutes to get to the basic realm of calm release. It helps us over- come the negative influences that we face with our hectic lifestyles.

Abdominal Breathing

A simple method of belly breathing is to utilize the diaphragm, located in the upper portion of the abdomen. A fundamental calm relaxing deep breath uses the upper abdominal muscles. This should be done at least 2 x per day.

Whole Body Release Technique

This constitutes pin pointing all areas of the body and utilizing relaxation methods to cover and focus on various body areas in order to release tension and stress. Usually commencing with the head area and all related muscles.

Excellent Technique for sleep therapy and pre surgery.

CHAPTER
5

Chapter 5

Choosing Fitness, Nutrition and Exercise

Healthy lifestyles and continued Fitness is our greatest National challenges. The cardinal rule is that it is always safest to check with your physician before starting any type of exercise or fitness program. Fitness and Nutrition work hand in hand, a program of safe simple weight loss through a basic nutrition plan combined with the appropriate fitness plan allows one to develop healthy lifestyle changes which will last for a life time.

There is now new research that suggests that mild, consistent exercise perhaps pushes the heart to make new blood vessels.

Everyone needs a Fitness Plan even those with Heart Disease. Remember as I pre-warned and especially heart patients talk to your doctor before starting a program.

One recent study in Germany studied several patients with serious heart failure. The patients' road bikes for as long as 30 minutes per day. It appeared that those individuals who were in the four month exercise program produced more new collateral vessels in their hearts than those that sat around most days.

CHOOSING FITNESS, NUTRITION AND EXERCISE

Maintaining a healthy mind and body by getting and staying in shape is essential. How do we start this wonderful journey toward developing and maintaining a healthy lifestyle?

The basic journey begins with eating well with wise food choices and reduced calorie intake and reduced portion size. Here are some easy steps to remember:

- The first thing to do is get the cake, cookies and chocolate out of the house

- Go through your kitchen cabinets, pantry and refrigerators and give away the tempting foods

- Get rid of foods that are going to be high calorie temptations

- When you have cleared out the foods that tend to promote fat, take an inventory of what is left

Stock your pantry or cabinets with items that can be easily prepared and that are healthy yet tasty:

- Whole Grain Pastas and Breads

- Diced tomatoes

- Black beans, kidney beans

- Canned chicken (low sodium or in water)

- Sun-dried tomatoes

- Mushrooms

- Fiber filled cereals

- Be sure and stock your refrigerator with many fresh fruits and vegetables

- Eat a lot of salads and add good lean protein to your salads, this assist you in eliminating hunger

The sugar free items assist you in lowering your sugar intake. Sugar free Jell-O and pudding are great for low or no sugar treats.

These healthy alternatives provide one of the easiest ways to lose weight. Fruits and vegetables are fabulous to assist you in lowering your appetite; you need at least 5 servings per day.

Remember to watch portion size and get 100 calorie snacks better yet WALK- you need around 5- 10,000 steps- 3 times a week to jump start your metabolism.

BASIC RECAP

Being in good shape is the best way to have a healthy active life.

BEGIN TODAY:

- Drink Water

- Eat fresh vegetables and fresh fruit everyday

- Avoid refined sugars

- Do abdominal crunches

- Do low back lifts

These have been a few fitness and nutrition tips that can help you sustain a healthy lifestyle.

CHAPTER

6

Chapter 6
Sharing the Spiritual Connection of Life & Health

Triumphant Over Fear of Loss

Emotional pain can often be more penetrating and piercing than physical pain. Early that morning I sat peering out the hospital window gazing at the snow. Sometimes too much knowledge is a true hinder. I was in that really dark place emotionally and hurt. Hurt to the core. My loss was grave. I had lost my third child, what I somehow knew was my third and last baby." The other two has been early in the pregnancy and I surely thought this one would make it. It was God's will and I was angry.

I thought my faith was solid. I had been proclaiming it for years. I soon discovered that I was not practicing what I preached, not just for days, weeks, or months, but years.

Every Mother's Day I was crushed. I soon realized how God truly works in mysterious ways.

My two nephews who I love as my own were charged to my watch by their mother who passed away at a very young age.

It was as if God had sent a heavenly replacement for my loss and my three angels were helping restore my faith. That faith that God will take care has come back time and time again. I have been blessed with several loving God children. Mother's Day is one of my favorites. The triumph over my fear of loss was guided by the restoration of my faith in God's will.

There is a smile in my soul because of a heart full of God's Children .....

"In The Nick of Time"

Perhaps, there have been times in your life when you have been convinced that God has given up on you. Unexplained illness can make you feel lost and sometimes forsaken. The more you attempt to care for and guard your health, the more certain things seem to break down. We sometimes want to give up.

Our attitude and attributes may actually pull us into what I call a spiritual decline. We set prayers aside, we cease placing God first in our life and health situations. We cease allowing God's vision to enter in the main things in our life. We start doing things by our own initiative without allowing God to come in. Now is the time we must beware of the tendency to question God with the "Why Me Lord". This is the place in our lives where we must be determined to act on faith.

We must have spiritual vitality, even when we don't have physical vitality. We must have spiritual freshness, even when we have clear physical decay.

This is the psychological place in our life where we must remember past blessings (such as) how angry we were with our mother when she picked us up at the drive-in and made us leave and go home with her. Our friend with whom we were to go home with was killed coming home in a fatal automobile crash. God was there in the nick of time.

This is the psychological place in our life where we must remember when we swerved to the left and the bus missed hitting the car, while the next car was hit killing many. God was there in the nick of time.

This is the psychological place in our life where we must remember the (sky way bridge) that gave way 30 minutes after you drove over the bridge.

This is the psychological place in our life where we must remember that the paramedics were located just next door when my heart stopped. God was there in the nick of time. This is the place in life where we must remember that we changed the airline ticket for a later flight and the one we were to take crashed in the Everglades. God was there in the nick of time.

This is the psychological place in our Life where we must remember that we have had:

A Life Time Filled, With an On Time God!

Health Wealth and Happiness God's Way (Proverbs 3:5)

Health can sometimes be an elusive state in its excellent form, but oh, is it worth fighting for? God reminds us that our body is our temple. It seems that we often forget that the mind is also a part of that temple and can be the controlling factor in our health status. It is wonderful if we learn early in life to care for our bodies and strive for a good healthy state. The realization that your mental health is just as important as your physical health is paramount in relieving stresses. If and when disease does attack that makes this the time to really understand and believe in the great power of God and His word. (Phil 4:4-7). That peace without understanding is surrounded by faith-the kind of faith that can move mountains and make tumors disappear. The health professionals are essential and you must assist them with your strong belief in knowing what God can do. Healing power is real.

The essential point to remember is that God never leaves us even if it is to assist us through a smooth transition in life's cycle.

Wealth has many faces. It is us who must gain the wisdom to recognize them. It is often thought to be loads of money or financial holdings that make us wealthy. Of course this is true. We would be remised not to acknowledge financial wealth. The real wealth however comes from your loved ones and friends, hugs, smiles, kisses, best wishes, letters, notes, cards, and the knowledge of God and His word. If we just take the time to savor a thank you, a call, or a chocolate bar because it is your favorite.

The big things are great also but if you just listen and become aware of all of the wonderful daily things occurring which confirms and reconfirms how really wealthy you are.

Happiness is often not understood. It really is peace of mind whatever state you are in. I don't mean you should not strive for excellence in that state. You must. But learn to handle the state and cope. I promise you that if you begin to take stock of all the really nice situations, nice people and blessings which occur in your life. God will grant you the happiness I am suggesting.

You will learn to love and be happy about the simplest things. The ability to walk out your door and drive to a job, think of those that cannot. The ability to walk a block, a mile, two miles. Oh WOW! Think of those that cannot. The ability to serve and get on your knees and truly know and thank God.

There are so many who lack this ability.

Oh let's look now to see how blessed we are with Health, Wealth and Happiness.

The Heart of Healing

Medicine is the art of healing but, knowing God is the heart of healing. Dear friends, what an exceptional privilege to share with you my thoughts about the power of God through His word and through focused prayer during the healing process.

Our world is turbulent, fast-paced and chaotic. Often either we or our family members need careful tending because of illness or potential illness. We must do everything medically feasible to determine the status of our medical condition, pinpointing the necessary test, procedures and course of care, to return us to maximum physical health.

I am a living witness that being a praying loving God and believing Christian matters in the healing process. Medical care and medicine works in my estimation much better if your mental attitude toward life and your trust in God serve as a partnership in concert with your medical professional skills.

You heal faster. The true scientist might not agree with me that trust and believing that God's healing process is valid. I believe that appreciating God's word and accepting His healing process does matter.

To me, being a loving and grateful person, appreciating this life God has given us and taking the time for the necessities of life are a part of the tending that we all need. If we choose to show and find what is beautiful rather than what is not. Life is ultimately better no matter what our physical state is. When we are physically drained, prayer helps to rebuild our strength and His powerful healing force replaces the drained forces with strong soothing power of love.

Open your mind, open your heart and choose to remind yourself and your loved ones who are the "Heart of Healing". I will say of the Lord, He is my refuge and my fortress, My God, in Him will I trust. Psalms 91:2

"Love, a Knock Out Prescription For The Spirit"

Galatians 5:22 "But the fruit of the Spirit is love, joy, peace, long suffering, gentleness, goodness, faith…John 15:12 "This is my commandment that ye love one another as I have love you". I am always amazed to watch the healing aspect of love especially through those who render and accept love by offering and receiving service during illness.

Real service is the outpouring and over flowing of a life full of love and devotion. It is an expression of God's nature and becomes a healing force for the mind and spirit of the giver and recipient.

I believe there is a phase during healing where along with medical technology that simple ordinary evidence of God and love becomes sure. If you are still enough and except God's will, His work will become evident. The ability to witness His true goodness will allow you to observe a miraculous and divine expression of the heart of our Lord Jesus Christ. God makes things clear within His work and we must just listen and find peace and comfort in knowing that He is always with us and His love for us is everlasting.

We honor God and are faithful to His loving spirit when we believe that He will take care of us.

He loved us so much He gave His son that we have everlasting life. Salvation is easy for us and we must remember that it cost God so much.

We must walk in his light and pass His love on to others. Pass His love on through the word and through deeds. Through love the Holy Spirit can guide us during times of stress and strain.

We need the grace of God to conquer and with- stand crisis. The requirements of God are not exceptional for His grace is simple. We must surrender and allow our faith to stand fast.

Once we begin to embrace God's grace and know the truth of His word, insight about stresses, strains and illnesses began to emerge. I believe this personal response to God is critical to healing mentally and physically. If God does not speak, nothing will happen. The really exciting revelation is that He always speaks; you must have the ability to hear.

God is wonderful in His relationship with you. He speaks in many different ways. In His healing He does not reveal His truth in the same way to all persons. He is creative. Often it seems He customizes His revelation for the individual. How awesome it is when you realize He is standing at the right hand of the doctor, the nurse, the lab tech, and the x-ray tech just when you need Him.

The understanding of a special intimacy with God has overwhelming power. Suddenly we come to a trust place of acceptance and enlightenment. Faith becomes natural, fear becomes manageable. Through the love of God we can help medicine work, nourish our body and our mind in our faith and realize that God has an amazing design to protect in different circumstances.

CHAPTER
7

Chapter 7
Preventing Aging-The Natural Way

The best instruction to patient and client regarding anti-aging falls into five fundamental.

Categories of Care:

a) Nutrition

b) Exercise/Fitness

c) Daily Routines

d) Stress Management

e) Supplementation

All the activities dealing with nutrition (calorie reduction), exercise/fitness and multi-vitamin supplement should only be initiated with the advice of physician.

Nutrition

This is the first line of defense against aging. The following are areas of concentration:

Lower the calorie intake to between 2000 – 3000 calories.

If obese follow a more restrictive calorie intake to be determined by body mass index (BMI) measurements e.g. the method which determines to total amount of body fat.

Lower your intake of saturated fats utilize mono- saturated fats only.

Exercise/Fitness

- All exercise programs should only be taken under the advice of your physician.

- Gentle walking is the best way to determine your fitness level, an early morning 15-20 minute walk should start your routine, gradually increasing the intensity and the length of the walk.

- Gentle weight training as tolerated should be introduced to your fitness program and should be done gradually.

Daily Routine

- The morning should start with a daily meditation routine, after a brisk 20-30min walk.

- The lunch period should be the most extensive meal for the day.

- The evening routine should include another mediation session, light dinner and prepare for bed early enough to get at least 7 hours of sleep.

Stress Management Techniques

- Stress Reduction is one of the main elements of the anti-aging process.

- Utilization of all the methods discussed earlier regarding stress relief is most important if you use them.

- Creative Imaginary

- Relaxation response skills

- Meditation several times daily

- Guided focused routines and tips

- Smoking cessation

- Brain wave technology

Preventive Supplements
(Physician prescribed or monitored)

Antioxidants

Natural food supplements

Multivitamins

Anti-aging techniques and skills can be learned and we can make these activities, skills and techniques an everyday part of our Healthy lifestyle.

Eating the proper types of food, remaining independent and making physical activity routines a part of our daily lives are the main ingredients for a better and enjoyable life.

CHAPTER

8

Chapter 8
Treasure the Breath-Taking Scenery of Life

In order to renew your mind, body and spirit you must find that peaceful, restful place within and find and experience your own true inner bliss and happiness. The ordinary treasures of life can often give us the happiest most joyful moments in our lives. The times when the sheer joy of seeing or hearing from a friend or loved one can bring you great joy.

The main ingredient of happiness comes from within, you must explore anything that is causing you to feel down or depressed. If possible get rid of it. If you cannot rid yourself of the stressor, then do everything you can to minimize its effect.

Our behavior can often dictate the status of our own happiness. Joy in our life has been found to clinically promote our brain functions to light up and become distressed, therefore laughter can scientifically cause a reduction in stress within individuals.

LEARN TO BE YOUR OWN LIFE COACH

You must assist your health professionals if you have a health concern. If you are problem free from infirmaries, learn to be your own health advocate.

There are three (3) main broad activities:

- Healthy eating

- Physical activity – increase and maintain muscle tone and endurance within your capabilities

- Make quality life style choices

Know that you are the most important person to be around for your family and friends. Your attitude means a lot.

The following thoughts will assist you in truly enjoying the breathtaking scenery of life:

- Learn to overcome obstacles, not dwell on them

- Take responsibility for your choices

- Change your life by not one thing or choice – it is many powerful choices per day

- Learn to make empowering choices

- Don't think in terms of how hard something might be but think of trying it just one more time

- Know that anything is possible

- Promote your own spiritual well being

- Don't miss out on learning opportunities, savor and treasure them

CHAPTER

9

CHAPTER 9
Admiring Life's View

If you have a strong desire to experience life's wonderful surroundings on a continuing basis with joy, then you must produce the results and basis for this experience from your choices or your reactions to those instances that are dealt to you.

Each of us has the power to fulfill a successful life purpose. There are certain success principles and strategies that can work in any endeavor we undertake.

The life principles are:

• Develop a life plan which offers (support, motivation, guidance, direction)

• Understand the value of others

• Identify, celebrate and be thankful for all good things within your life

• Take action steps to carry out the lifelong plan as you achieve your short term and long term goals, you will need often to review, access and modify these goals

• Be prepared to change your actions if needed in order to experience desired results and experience personal success

- Connect with positive pleasant relationships

- Maintain your spiritual faith, peace with and thru God

Say yes and treat yourself—accept you are human and know that human emotions are necessary.

GIVE

- Give of yourself your time and

- Generosity allows us to feel that we matter in this life and it is the bridge thru love to the connection of others that empowers us the most

- As you admire life's view from a healthy life style perspective.

- Know the strength in the power of prayer

- To maintain a balance in the mind, body and spirit you must treat others around you with kindness, compassion and with love. If this is done you will keep life's greatest benefits.

- Learn to let your spirit fly- laughter is a sure way to let your spirit soar

- Magnificently impressive musical allures or entertainment for your senses from all genre's-

Open up your mind and listen

- If you really love life as I do you can remember your most blissful and happiest moments.

- When you get blue, just remember your happiest moments

   Remember how you felt when things felt right, special, easy and good.

   Remember a great sound or song that you loved.

   Remember there is only one life-LIVE IT,
   LOVE IT AND YOU CAN MAKE IT, SO IT DOESN'T
   GET ANY BETTER THAN THIS!!!!!

About the Author

Dr. Ruth Joyce Colbert Barnes RN, PhD is the Principal and CEO of the Colbert Enterprise Inc. and the Chief Medical Research Consultant for the Colbert Group.

She is nationally recognized for her collaboration with Medical Researchers and Healthcare Providers while also working closely in the Business and Education community. She has been a former City Official and City Manager.

Throughout her professional career she has always known and expressed a keen interest in the healing relationship between mind, body, and the spiritual connection as a Compliment Therapy to Traditional Therapies.

Dr. Barnes has known that the mind has always been there to be served by the body. It produces intellectual powers that have great strength and healing capabilities which can clearly assist the traditional methodologies. This book is filled with light hearted lifestyle management advice. Dr. Barnes has the ability to inspire and motivate others to adhere to a great healthy lifestyle.

To obtain information about enjoying Dr. Barnes as a consultant, Lifestyle Practioner, Coach or to give this book as a gift to someone......

Please see
email dr.ruthcolbertbarnes@yahoo.com for additional copies.